Rookie
Read-About®
Science

Amazing Mammals

by Lisa M. Herrington

Content Consultant
Dr. Lucy Spelman
Zoological Medicine Specialist

Reading Consultant
Jeanne M. Clidas, Ph.D.
Reading Specialist

Children's Press®
An Imprint of Scholastic Inc.

Library of Congress Cataloging-in-Publication Data
Herrington, Lisa M., author.
Amazing mammals/by Lisa M. Herrington.
   pages cm. — (Rookie read about science. Strange animals)
Summary: "Introduces the reader to amazing animals." —Provided by publisher.
Includes index.
ISBN 978-0-531-22600-1 (library binding) — ISBN 978-0-531-22746-6 (pbk.)
   1. Mammals—Miscellanea—Juvenile literature. 2. Children's questions and answers.
I. Title.
QL706.2.H47 2016
   599.02—dc23   2015021143

Produced by Spooky Cheetah Press
Design by Keith Plechaty

Printed in China 62

SCHOLASTIC, CHILDREN'S PRESS, ROOKIE READ-ABOUT®, and associated logos
are trademarks and/or registered trademarks of Scholastic Inc.

2 3 4 5 6 7 8 9 10 R 25 24 23 22 21 20 19 18 17 16

Photographs ©: cover: Steve Bloom Images/Superstock, Inc.; 3 top left: Patryk
Kosmider/Shutterstock, Inc.; 3 top right: Neirfy/Shutterstock, Inc.; 3 bottom: Anan
Kaewkhammul/Shutterstock, Inc.; 4: age fotostock/Superstock, Inc.; 7: NHPA/
Superstock, Inc.; 8: Suzi Eszterhas/Minden Pictures; 11: Tony Camacho/Science
Source; 12: Minden Pictures/Superstock, Inc.; 15: Patrick Shyu/National Geographic
Creative; 16 left: J & C Sohns/Superstock, Inc.; 16 center, 16 right: Tier und
Naturfotografie/Superstock, Inc.; 19: Ken Catania/Visuals Unlimited; 20 top: Roland
Seitre/Minden Pictures; 20 bottom: Kristian Bell/Shutterstock, Inc.; 23 main: John
Warden/Superstock, Inc.; 23 inset: louise murray/Alamy Images; 24: Brian J. Skerry/
National Geographic Creative; 26: Efired/Shutterstock, Inc.; 27: Mint Images/
Superstock, Inc.; 28 background, 29 background: Zack Frank/Shutterstock, Inc.; 28
top: Animals Animals/Superstock, Inc.; 28 bottom: age fotostock/Superstock, Inc.;
29 top: NaturePL/Superstock, Inc.; 29 center: Denis Palanque/Biosphoto; 29 bottom
left: Biosphoto/Superstock, Inc.; 29 bottom right: Amy Harris/Dreamstime; 30:
imageBROKER/Superstock, Inc.; 31 top: Tony Camacho/Science Source; 31 center
top: Biosphoto/Superstock, Inc.; 31 center bottom: Minden Pictures/Superstock, Inc.;
31 bottom: Patrick Shyu/National Geographic Creative.

Table of Contents

That's Amazing!

Mammals are some of the world's most amazing animals. People, dogs, and cats are all mammals. So are bears, elephants, and lions. There are many unusual mammals, too. The pangolin looks like a pinecone that walks. And it plays a strange trick!

When it is in danger, a pangolin rolls its body into a ball. Now it is protected from **predators**. They cannot get past the pangolin's hard scales. Like a skunk, this animal can also release a stinky smell.

7

What Makes a Mammal a Mammal?

most give birth to live young

breathes air through lungs

has a backbone

makes milk to feed young

warm-blooded

has fur or hair

8

Pangolins are the only mammals covered in scales. But all mammals have fur. That includes hair and whiskers. Mammals also have backbones and are warm-blooded. Almost all mammals give birth to live young. And they make milk for their babies.

Koalas have large noses that let them smell which leaves are safe to eat.

Mammals Up High

Bats are the only mammals that can fly. They are **nocturnal**. They sleep hanging upside down during the day. At night, they look for food.

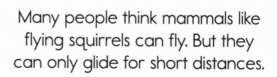

FUN FACT!

Many people think mammals like flying squirrels can fly. But they can only glide for short distances.

Flying foxes are the largest types of bats.

Sloths live in the rain forest. They hang upside down in the trees and rarely come down. They eat, sleep, and give birth in trees. They use their curved claws to hold on to branches. Sloths sleep up to 20 hours a day. They move so little that small plants called algae grow on their fur.

FUN FACT!

Sloths are the world's slowest mammals. Cheetahs are the fastest. A cheetah can run as fast as a car travels on a highway.

Cool Primates

Monkeys belong to a group of mammals called **primates**. Most primates live where it is warm. Snow monkeys live in mountains in Japan. Their bodies are made for the cold and snow. In the winter, their fur grows thicker. These playful monkeys like to make snowballs for fun. They also jump in hot springs to stay warm.

Snow monkeys are
a type of Japanese
macaque (muh-KAK).

Lemurs are primates, too.
Most of them look pretty unusual.
But sifakas (sih-FA-kahs) are oddest
of all. When they travel on the
ground, sifakas hop sideways
on their two legs. They look like
they are dancing!

What a Nose!

Moles spend most of their lives underground. Their bodies are made for digging. The star-nosed mole's nose is made up of 22 pink fingerlike parts. It helps the mole move through the dirt to catch worms, insects, and other **prey**.

The star-nosed mole is the world's
fastest-eating mammal. It can finish
its food in less than a second.

platypus

spiny anteater

The platypus is another mammal with a strange snout. Like a duck, it has a bill. The platypus uses its bill to hunt insects and small fish. It spends much of its time in water. It uses its webbed feet to swim.

The platypus is one of only two mammals that lay eggs. The spiny anteater, or echidna (eh-KID-nah), is the other. All other mammals give birth to live young.

FUN FACT!

The male platypus is the most venomous mammal. It has a poison spike inside each ankle. It uses the spikes for self-defense.

Ocean Mammals

This beluga (beh-LOO-gah) whale lives in the water. But it is not a fish! All whales and dolphins are mammals. Mammals breathe air with their lungs. Like all ocean mammals, the beluga has to come to the water's surface for air. It breathes through the blowhole on the top of its head.

A blowhole is a whale's nose.

The manatee is another strange sea mammal. It breathes through its nostrils. It must come to the water's surface to take a breath. Manatees are also called sea cows. Manatees, like all mammals, have hair. It is just hard to see!

There is no doubt about it. Mammals really are amazing!

Sailors once thought manatees were mermaids!

Which Is Stranger?

tarsier

- Although the tarsier (TAR-see-ehr) cannot move its huge eyes, it can turn its head backward.

- Special finger pads and toe pads help tarsiers hold on to branches.

- This shy primate is about the size of a squirrel.

You Decide!

naked mole rat

- Naked mole rats do not need much hair. The underground tunnels where they live are warm. And they do not need hair to protect their bodies from the sun.

- Mole rats are not entirely naked. They have about 100 fine hairs on their bodies. The hairs act like whiskers so they can feel around in the dark.

- Naked mole rats eat their own poop. It helps them digest their food.

TOP 5 Facts
About Mammals

1. Mammals are found on every continent and in every ocean.

2. There are more than 5,000 kinds of mammals.

3. Mammals that grow in their mothers' pouches are marsupials. They include koalas, kangaroos, and opossums—the only marsupials that live in the U.S.

4. Most mammals are good parents. They care for their young and teach them how to survive on their own.

5. Mammals eat a wide variety of foods. They eat meat, plants, or both. Pandas, for example, eat mostly bamboo in the forests of China.

Record Holders

Largest
A blue whale is longer than a basketball court and weighs as much as 15 buses.

Smallest
The Etruscan shrew is small enough to fit on a spoon!

Longest Tongue
The giant anteater has no teeth. It uses its long tongue to slurp up more than 30,000 ants a day!

Tallest
A giraffe is as tall as a two-story building.

Animal CRACK-UPS

Is that a giant walking mop? No! This shaggy dog is a Komondor. The Komondor watches over sheep. Its heavy coat helps it blend in with the flock. The Komondor's coat also protects it from bad weather and enemies.

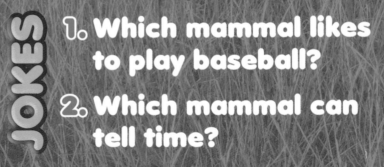

JOKES

1. **Which mammal likes to play baseball?**

2. **Which mammal can tell time?**

Answers: 1. A bat! 2. A watchdog!

Glossary

nocturnal (nok-TUR-nuhl): active at night

predators (PRED-uh-turs): animals that hunt other animals for food

prey (PRAY): animals that are hunted for food

primates (PRYE-mates): animal group that includes humans, monkeys, and apes

Index

Facts for Now

Visit this Scholastic Web site for more information on mammals:
www.factsfornow.scholastic.com
Enter the keyword **Mammals**

About the Author

Lisa M. Herrington loves writing books about animals for kids. She lives in Trumbull, Connecticut, with her husband, Ryan, and daughter, Caroline.